NAIL CHARMS

BY THE EDITORS OF KLUTZ

KLUTZ

CONTENTS

CHARMING DESIGNS

WATERMELON 23	**STRAWBERRY** 24	**PINEAPPLE** 26	**FRUITY FIZZ** 27	**ZIPPER** 28	**LEOPARD SPOTS** 29

GINGHAM 30	**DAISY** 31	**BUTTON SHIRT** 32	**ARGYLE** 33	**SUGAR SKULL** 34	**LACE** 35

PENGUIN 36	**CRITTER CUTIE** 37	**NESTING DOLL** 38	**FLOWER BASKET** 39	**UNICORN** 40	**PRINCESS** 41

GALAXY 42	**UFO** 43	**CHEESEBURGER** 44	**FRIES** 45	**DONUT** 46	**CUPCAKE** 47

BEACH 48	**SUMMER** 50	**WINTER** 51	**OWL** 52	**BUTTERFLY** 53	**OCTOPUS** 54

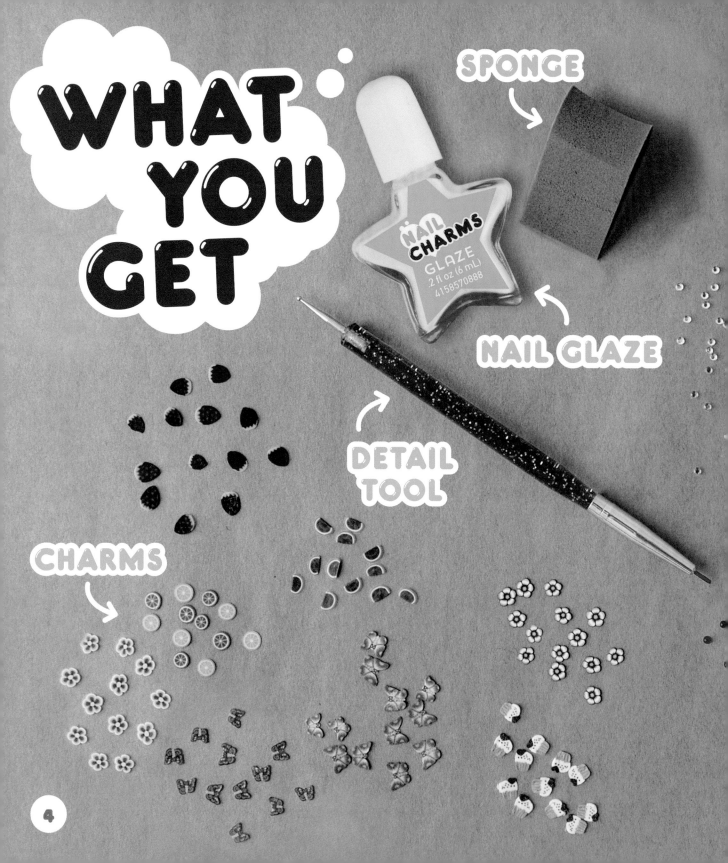

WHAT YOU GET

SPONGE

NAIL CHARMS GLAZE
2 fl oz (6 mL)
4158570888

NAIL GLAZE

DETAIL TOOL

CHARMS

4

MINI PEARLS AND GEMS

GLITTER

WHAT YOU'LL NEED

✓ Nail polish in different colors

✓ Non-acetone nail polish remover

✓ Nail clippers

✓ Cotton pads or balls

✓ Paper towels

✓ Scrap paper

✓ Scissors

STUDS

NAIL TAPE

PUFFY CHARMS

GETTING STARTED

Keep reading for important info about the instructions in this book and how to set up your workspace.

ABOUT THE ART

You might notice that the step-by-step illustrations in this book are upside down. This is because the designs are meant to appear right side up to the people checking out your manicure. The art shows you what your nails look like as you paint them with your hand flat on the table.

You'll probably need help painting the nails on your writing hand. So team up with your BFF or an adult for your manicure session.

Tip

Tip
Base

If you want the designs to face you, you can turn the book upside down so the designs are upright.

NAIL POLISH COLORS

You'll use your own colored nail polish to paint the designs in this book. To keep things easy, the instructions will tell you to use specific colors. But feel free to change them to make your manicure your own. In case you need some ideas, the colors shown above will show off your charms and gems.

SET UP YOUR STUDIO

Cover a flat work surface (like a table or desk) with newspaper or scrap paper. Gather your nail polish, nail glaze, and tool so that they're nearby but not so close that you might knock them over as you work. You can keep your charms and gems in a small dish so they don't get lost. You'll also need a few cotton balls or pads, some nail polish remover, and a sheet of paper to make a palette (page 10).

Tips to Keep in Mind

* Paint one nail with the nail glaze to make sure you don't have an allergic reaction. If you develop a rash, remove the polish immediately with non-acetone nail polish remover. See a doctor if the problem continues.

* Only paint glaze on your nails, not your skin. Don't paint over open cuts or wounds.

* Don't eat the glaze or give it to someone who might. Also, keep your supplies away from young children and pets.

* If you spill the glaze, wipe it up right away with a wet paper towel.

GIVE YOURSELF A MANICURE

A simple manicure preps your nail for the base coat and charm designs. If you want to skip this step and paint on a base coat right away, that's fine, too.

WHAT YOU NEED

- Cotton balls or pads
- Non-acetone nail polish remover
- Nail brush
- Nail clippers
- Nail file
- Nail buffer
- Small bowl of warm water
- Olive oil
- Lotion

1. CLEAN

Remove any old polish from your nails, and wash your hands with warm, soapy water. Clean under your nails—you can use a nail brush if you'd like.

2. TRIM

Trim your nails with clippers so they're all about the same length. It's easier to make designs if your nails are long, so don't cut them too short.

3. FILE

Place a nail file just under the edge of your nail. Hold it at a 45-degree angle and make long, even strokes.

Rounded   Square

For a **rounded shape**, file from the corners toward the center to create a curved edge. For a **square shape**, file straight across your nail in one direction, then round the corners.

4. BUFF

Your buffer should have a rough side (to smooth) and a softer side (to shine). Make light strokes over your nail with the rough side to get rid of bumps or ridges. Then use the soft side to create shine.

When you're using a nail file or buffer, make long, even strokes in one direction—don't saw back and forth.

5. SOAK

If you want to push back your cuticles, soak your fingertips in a bowl of warm water for about 5 minutes. Massage a little olive oil into your cuticles and use your thumb to gently push them back. Wash your hands with soap to remove the oil.

6. MOISTURIZE

Rub some lotion into your hands (but not your nails). Wait about 10 minutes for the lotion to soak in.

Be 100% You

Everyone's nails are different, so don't worry if the designs don't look exactly like the ones in this book. Feel free to adjust the designs so they look the best on you.

HOW TO PAINT A BASE COAT

Before you start adding charms, nail tape, or glitter, paint on a base coat.

1

Dip the brush into the nail polish bottle. Wipe the sides of the brush against the inside of the bottle lip to remove extra polish. There should be a thin coat of polish on the brush, but it shouldn't be drippy.

2

Make a stripe in the middle of your nail. Start at the base of your nail and brush toward the tip.

3

Paint another stripe on the left side of the nail . . . and then the right side. Let the polish dry.

4

Repeat Steps 1–3 if you want a second coat. Let it dry completely.

Keep your hand flat on the table while you work.

Drying Time

It usually takes 3–4 minutes for polish to dry. A thicker coat will take longer to dry. To speed up drying, use a blow-dryer on the cool setting.

USING YOUR TOOL

You'll use your tool to paint tiny designs with nail polish. It has two ends: a dotter and a detail brush. Before you try making designs from this book, read pages 10–13 and practice using your tool on a piece of paper.

The **DOTTER** helps you paint dots and other shapes. It's also handy when you're adding charms and jewels.

The **DETAIL BRUSH** lets you paint fancy designs and apply glaze.

MAKING A PALETTE

Instead of dipping your tool directly into a polish bottle, you'll work from a paper palette.

1

Fold a piece of paper in half. Put one drop of polish on the paper by letting it drip off the brush.

2

Hold the tool like a pen. Dip the tip of the detail brush or the dotter into the polish. The tip should be covered, but not too globby. If you're using the brush, twirl it slowly in the polish so the bristles make a point.

If the polish dries up or gets sticky, add a fresh drop to the palette.

NAIL BASICS

Mix and match these accent nail designs with the charm designs on pages 23–55 to make a manicure that's perfectly on point.

TOOL BASICS

Here are some basic shapes that you can make with the dotter and the detail brush on your tool.

You can also use your detail brush to draw shapes, if that's easier for you.

MAKING DOTS

1
Dip your dotter into a drop of nail polish on your palette (page 10). The dotter tip should be covered, but not dripping.

2
Lightly press the dotter tip of the tool to your nail, then lift it up.

MAKING SHAPES

1
Dip the dotter into polish. Then draw the outline of the shape you want on your nail.

2
Fill in the shape by dabbing nail polish inside of it with the dotter.

For really round dots, re-dip the dotter in the polish for each new dot.

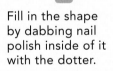

MAKING LINES

Dip your detail brush or your dotter in polish. Make a smooth swipe across your nail to draw a line. Your first few tries might look a little bumpy—but just keep practicing, and you'll get even lines in no time.

Detail brush

Dotter

Cleaning the Tool

Be sure to clean the tool when you switch colors and when you're finished with your charm designs. Keep your cleaning supplies handy since you'll need to clean the tool often.

DOTTER

Moisten a cotton pad or ball with nail polish remover. Wipe the dotter on the damp cotton until it's totally clean.

DETAIL BRUSH

Carefully pour a little nail polish remover into an old bottle cap. (If you need help, get an adult to do it.) Swish your brush bristles in the cap to clean it, and then wipe the brush on a paper towel so it stays pointy. Change the liquid in the cap every now and then.

Be sure your nail polish remover is non-acetone or it will make the brush bristles fall out.

ADDING GEMS & CHARMS

You'll use nail glaze to attach charms, mini pearls, and gems to your nails.

1

If your nails are painted, make sure that they're dry. Brush on a thin layer of nail glaze.

2

Place the charms or gems you want on your nail, and press them lightly so that they stick. Let them dry for 2 minutes so they set.

3

Paint over the top of the charms and gems with another thin coat of glaze. Let the nail dry.

Sticking to It

When you're finished with your manicure, treat your nails gently. To make your designs last longer, use clear nail polish instead of glaze. And if you're doing a fancy design for a special occasion, it's better to do your nails the same day so that they'll look their best.

If you don't want to paint on a second coat of glaze, use the detail brush to add glaze around the edges of the charms so that they stick.

To remove your charms, place a cotton pad soaked in remover over your nail and let it sit for a minute or two. It might take some rubbing to remove gems and mini pearls. For flatter charms, gently peel them off after they've loosened.

USING NAIL TAPE

Use nail tape to create thin stripes and patterns.

If the end of the tape gets crinkled as you pull it from the roll, just snip it off before you apply it to your nail.

1
Find the end of the nail tape roll. Cut a piece of nail tape slightly wider or longer than your nail.

2
The back of the tape is sticky. Press the tape onto your nail—you can use the dotter tool to press it down, too.

3
Trim the tape ends with nail clippers. Cut as close as possible to the nail.

4
Use the dotter to tuck the ends of the tape into the sides of your nail.

5
Brush a thin coat of nail glaze over the entire nail, including the tape.

FINISHED NAIL

NAIL TAPE STENCILS

You can also use nail tape as a stencil and paint over it to create clean lines. Be sure that your base coat is totally dry before you start.

1
Cut two pieces of nail tape. You want the tape to be a little wider than your nail so that you can peel it off later. Press it firmly onto the nail so that polish doesn't get underneath.

2
Paint over the tape with polish.

3
While the polish is still wet, peel the tape off to reveal your design.

4
Brush a thin coat of nail glaze over the entire nail.

Peeling the tape off while the polish is still wet keeps the stencil lines crisp.

USING GLITTER

Use your glaze and your glitter pot to make a glittered nail.

1
Paint your nail a solid color. Brush a thin layer of nail glaze onto your nail.

2
While your nail is still wet, roll it in the pot of glitter. Roll it back and forth until the nail is covered.

3
Use your tool to brush off any extra glitter. Pat your nail lightly so the glitter lies evenly. Let it dry for a few minutes.

4
Gently brush glaze over the glitter on your nail. If you need to, wipe your glaze brush on a paper towel to remove the glitter.

To remove glitter from your nails, wipe it off using a cotton pad soaked in nail polish remover. Glitter is stubborn, so it may take a little while to come off.

GLITTER ♡ SHAPES

Glitter can also be used to make cute shapes and symbols on your nails.

1

Dip the dotter or the detail brush in nail polish or glaze and draw a shape, like a heart, on your nail.

2

Immediately roll your nail in the pot of glitter so that it sticks to the wet glaze.

3

Wipe off your tool and use it to knock off any extra glitter. Pat your nail lightly so the glitter lies evenly. Let it dry for a few minutes.

4

Gently brush glaze over the glitter on your nail. The glaze may take longer than usual to dry.

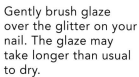

GLITTER FADE

Create this glitter effect by using the sponge included with this book.

1 Paint a small amount of glaze onto the sponge.

2 Pour a little glitter onto a plate. Dip the sponge, glaze side down, in the glitter.

3 Press the sponge to the base of your nail.

4 Without adding more glitter to the sponge, press it to your nail again while moving it toward the tip so that the glitter fades out.

5 Brush on a coat of nail glaze and let it dry.

OMBRÉ

You can use your sponge and nail polish to create this cool color effect.

1

Paint a base coat onto your nails and let it dry. Place strips of Scotch tape around your nail. This will keep the polish on your nail instead of your finger.

2

Paint different-colored stripes of polish onto the sponge. You'll need to use a lot of polish, so be generous.

3

Roll the sponge back and forth over your nail. Do not wipe or rub, as this will smudge the stripes together. Just keep rolling until it looks the way you want.

4

Slowly remove the tape. Dip your detail brush in nail polish remover and use it to clean up the edges.

5

Brush a clear coat of glaze over the entire nail and let it dry.

Cleaning the Sponge

To clean your sponge, just cut off the dirty parts with scissors to get a new flat surface. If you use up your sponge, you can use cosmetic sponges, sold at drugstores.

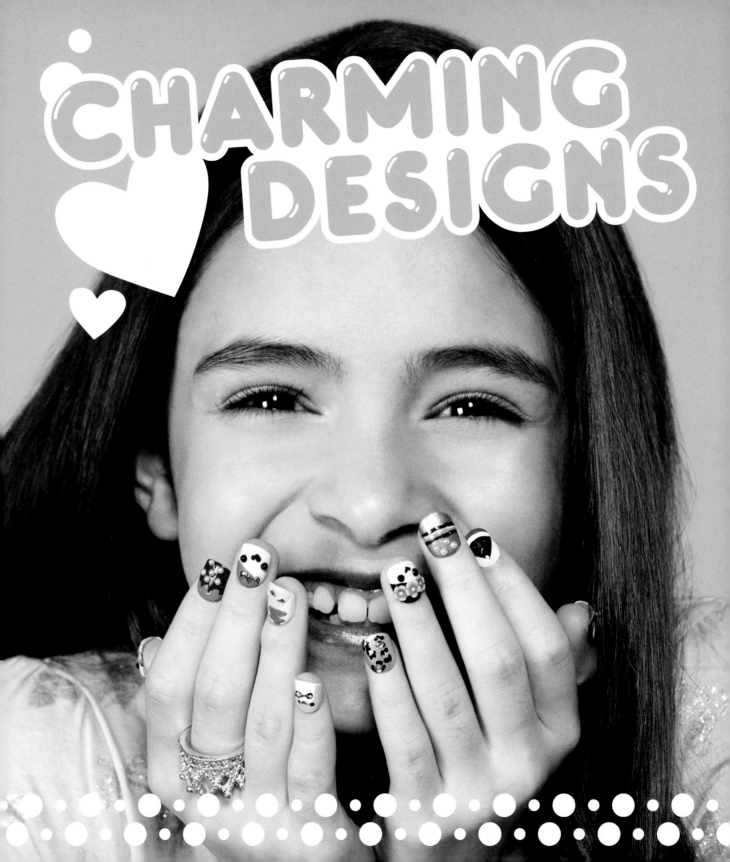

WATERMELON

WHAT YOU'LL NEED

- 4 colors of polish
- Nail tool
- Nail glaze
- Mini black pearls
- Nail tape
- Nail clippers

1
Paint your nail a solid color. Let it dry completely.

2
Use two pieces of nail tape to make a triangle shape.

3
Paint a red triangle shape. Remove the nail tape while the polish is still wet.

4
Paint a thick white stripe at the tip of your nail.

5
Paint a thin green stripe at the very tip of your nail.

6
Use glaze to attach mini black pearls for seeds.

STRAWBERRY

WHAT YOU'LL NEED

2 colors of polish • Nail tool
• Mini white pearls • Nail glaze

1

Paint your nail
a solid color.

2

Use the tool to
paint leaves at the
base of the nail.

3

Attach mini
pearls with nail
glaze for seeds.

THE COMPLETE LOOK

P. 30

Check out this
section to see
how you can mix
and match your
nail designs
and puffy
charms.

PINEAPPLE

1

Paint your nail a solid color.

2

Paint a yellow oval shape for the fruit.

3

Draw spiky leaves at the base.

4

Attach triangle studs with nail glaze.

THE COMPLETE LOOK

P. 18

FRUITY FIZZ

WHAT YOU NEED
2 colors of polish • Nail tool • Citrus slice charms • Gems • Nail glaze

1

Paint your nail a solid color.

2

Make a white cloud shape at the base of the nail for foam.

3

Use the dotter to make dots in orange and white for bubbles.

4

Attach gems and citrus slice charms with glaze.

THE COMPLETE LOOK

P. 17

WHAT YOU'LL NEED

3 colors of polish • Nail tool
• Nail tape • Gem • Nail glaze

ZIPPER

THE COMPLETE LOOK

P. 29

1 Paint your nail a solid color.

2 Using a different color, paint a triangle shape at the nail base. Let it dry.

3 Use three pieces of nail tape (page 16) to make a Y shape.

4 Using the tool, make a teardrop shape with silver polish for the zipper pull. Add dots around the tape for zipper teeth.

5 Attach a white gem to the point of the teardrop. Add a black dot to the center of the teardrop.

LEOPARD SPOTS

WHAT YOU'LL NEED

- 3 colors of polish
- Nail tool
- Gems
- Nail glaze

1

Paint your nail a solid color.

2

Using white polish, make different-sized spots on your nail.

3

Use the dotter to make black C shapes around each spot.

4

Use nail glaze to attach gems to the center of a few spots.

GINGHAM

WHAT YOU'LL NEED

3 colors of polish • Nail tool • Black mini pearls • Nail glaze

1 Paint your nail a solid color.

2 Make three light-pink stripes from top to bottom.

3 Make four light-pink stripes that go across the nail.

4 Using the dotter, place a dot of deep pink where the stripes cross each other.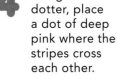

5 For a picnic-themed nail, use nail glaze to attach mini pearls for ants.

1 Paint your nail a solid color.

 2 Using white polish, make a dot in the center.

 3 Using the tool, paint a petal.

4 Make another petal on the opposite side of the dot.

 5 Make petals on the left and right sides of the dot.

6 Add four more petals. Use nail glaze to attach a gem in the center of the daisy.

WHAT YOU'LL NEED
2 colors of polish • Nail tool • Gem • Nail glaze

DAISY

THE COMPLETE LOOK

  P. 17 P. 41 P. 21

WHAT YOU'LL NEED

3 colors of polish • Nail tool
• Mini pearls • Nail glaze

THE COMPLETE LOOK

BUTTON SHIRT

1

Paint your nail a solid color.

2

Paint a white collar around the nail base.

3

Paint a pink oval at the base for the neckline.

4

Add mini pearls with nail glaze for buttons.

ARGYLE

1
Paint your nail a solid color.

2
Make an X with two pieces of nail tape.

3
Paint the left side of the X pink and the right side of the X red. Remove the tape.

4
Using the dotter, form a diamond shape in the center.

5
Extend the dotted lines to make half-diamonds on the left and right sides.

Remember to remove the tape while the polish is still wet.

SUGAR SKULL

1 Paint your nail a solid color.

2 Using the dotter, make dots to paint a purple flower for each eye.

3 Use the dotter to draw a heart for the nose. Add dots at the tip to make teeth.

4 To finish your skull, attach two gems for eyes and a flower charm with nail glaze.

LACE

WHAT YOU'LL NEED

2 colors of polish · 2 mini pearls · Nail glaze

1
Paint your nail a solid color.

2
Make three white dots at the tip of your nail to form a cloverleaf shape.

3
Draw three white half-circles below the cloverleaf.

4
Add another layer of white half-circles. Make three blue dots on the cloverleaf shape.

5
Make three white dots on the edge of the design. Use nail glaze to attach two mini pearls.

THE COMPLETE LOOK

WHAT YOU'LL NEED

- 3 colors of polish
- Nail tool
- Triangle stud
- 2 teardrop gems
- Nail glaze

PENGUIN

1

Paint your nail a solid color.

2

Start at the tip of your nail and draw a white half-oval.

3

Make two black dots for eyes.

4

Use nail glaze to attach a triangle stud for a beak and two teardrop gems for a bow tie.

WHAT YOU'LL NEED

4 colors of polish • Nail tool
• 3 mini pearls • Nail glaze

CRITTTER CUTIE

To make different critters, just change the ears! Paint long, thin ears for a bunny or small, round ears for a chipmunk.

THE COMPLETE LOOK

1 Paint your nail a solid color. Make a white half-circle at the tip.

2 Paint over the white half-circle with orange. (The white layer makes the orange brighter.)

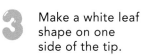

3 Make a white leaf shape on one side of the tip.

4 Paint another white leaf shape on the other side of the tip.

5 Paint two pointy orange ears. Make two pink dots for cheeks.

6 Use glaze to attach two black mini pearls for eyes and a pink mini pearl for a nose.

NESTING DOLL

THE COMPLETE LOOK

P. 31   P. 39

1 Paint your nail a solid color. Let it dry completely.

2 Make an upside down V shape in the center of your nail with two pieces of tape.

3 Paint the bottom half pink. Remove the tape.

Remember to remove the nail tape while the polish is still wet.

4 Using a different color, draw a sideways oval inside the pink shape.

5 Use the dotter to add black eyes and hair. Make white dots for a collar.

6 Attach two teardrop gems at the point of the collar with glaze.

FLOWER BASKET

WHAT YOU'LL NEED
4 colors of polish • Nail tool • 3 flower charms • Nail glaze

1 Paint your nail a solid color.

2 Paint the top half of your nail white. Curve the bottom of this shape a little.

3 Brush yellow polish over the white shape. (The white helps the yellow show up better.)

4 With the tool, add brown lines over the yellow shape to make a grid.

5 Attach the flower charms below the basket with nail glaze.

THE COMPLETE LOOK

P. 17

UNICORN

WHAT YOU'LL NEED

4 colors of polish • Nail tool • Black mini pearl
• Teardrop gem • Nail glaze

1
Paint your nail a solid color.

2
Draw a white circle in the center.

3
Make one side of the circle pointy for the chin. Add ears and a half-oval for the body.

4
Use aqua polish to draw the mane.

5
Add a light pink dot for a cheek.

6
Attach a black mini pearl and a teardrop gem with glaze for the eye and the horn.

THE COMPLETE LOOK

P. 17   P. 53   P. 18

40

WHAT YOU'LL NEED

- 5 colors of polish
- Nail tool
- Nail glaze
- Black mini pearls
- 3 teardrop gems

THE COMPLETE LOOK

PRINCESS

1

Paint your nail a solid color for the face.

2

On the base of your nail, make a swipe of light blue.

3

Add a swipe of teal that goes across the entire base of your nail.

4

Use the dotter to paint a red heart shape for lips and two pink dots for cheeks.

5

Attach two black mini pearls for eyes and three teardrop gems for a tiara.

GALAXY

WHAT YOU'LL NEED

- 2 colors of polish
- Nail tool
- Glitter
- Gem
- Star stud
- Nail glaze

1

Paint your nail a solid color.

2

Use your detail brush to paint stripes of glaze on your nail.

3

While the glaze is still wet, roll your nail in glitter to make glitter stripes.

4

Using the dotter, make white dots for stars. Use glaze to attach a star stud and a gem for a planet.

Use a glittery nail polish as a base coat to add even more sparkle.

WHAT YOU'LL NEED

3 colors of polish • Glitter • Nail tool • Nail tape • Gem • Nail glaze

UFO

1 Paint your nail a solid color. Let it dry completely.

2 Make a narrow X with two pieces of nail tape.

3 Paint yellow polish on the top part of the X and remove the tape. Roll your nail in glitter while the polish is still wet.

4 Draw a silver fan shape below the glitter triangle.

5 Round the point of the fan with silver polish.

6 Add three black dots for windows.

7 Attach a gem on the dome of the UFO with nail glaze.

THE COMPLETE LOOK

CHEESEBURGER

WHAT YOU'LL NEED

6 colors of polish • Nail tool • White mini pearls • Nail glaze

1
Paint your nail gold.

2
Paint a wide white stripe across your nail.

3
Paint thin red, green, yellow, and dark brown stripes over the white stripe.

If your nail is small, skip some topping stripes to save space.

4
Use the detail brush to add a wavy edge for the lettuce.

5
Attach mini white pearls at the base for sesame seeds.

THE COMPLETE LOOK

P. 45   P. 27

44

WHAT YOU'LL NEED
2 colors of polish • Nail tool
• Nail tape • Nail glaze
• Nail clippers

FRIES

1

Paint your nails
a solid red.

2

Draw thin yellow
stripes on the
base of the nail
for fries.

3

Paint over the
ends of the fries
with a curved
red shape.

4

Place a piece of
nail tape near the
tip of the nail.

5

Trim the ends of
the tape with nail
clippers. Paint your
nail with glaze to
seal in the tape.

WHAT YOU'LL NEED

- 3 colors of polish
- Nail tool
- 3 gems
- Nail glaze

THE COMPLETE LOOK

DONUT

1 Paint your nail a solid color.

2 Make a peach C shape in the corner of the nail tip.

3 Paint a wavy white stripe inside the peach shape for frosting.

4 Attach gems with nail glaze for sprinkles.

CUPCAKE

WHAT YOU'LL NEED
5 colors of polish • Nail tool • Mini pearls • Nail glaze

1
Paint your nails a solid color.

2
From the tip, make three stripes halfway down the nail.

3
Paint the base of the nail white for frosting.

4
Use the dot tool to add cheek dots and a mouth.

5
Attach mini pearls with glaze for eyes and sprinkles.

If you want to keep your cupcake design simple, skip the face.

THE COMPLETE LOOK

47

BEACH

WHAT YOU NEED

2 colors of polish • Sponge • Glitter • Nail tool • Gems • Star stud • Nail glaze

1

Paint your nails a solid color.

2

Paint the top half of your nail white.

3

Use the detail brush to make a white squiggle.

4

Let the white polish dry a little. Then blot it with the sponge to blend the colors.

5

Paint glaze at the tip of your nail and then quickly roll it in glitter for sand.

6

Use glaze to attach gems and a star stud for a starfish.

Add critters to your beach! Use red polish to make a simple crab with black mini pearls for eyes.

SUMMER

1
Paint your nails a solid color. Make an ombré fade with three colors and a sponge (page 21).

2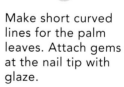
Paint a thin curved line down your nail.

3
Make short curved lines for the palm leaves. Attach gems at the nail tip with glaze.

WHAT YOU'LL NEED
4 colors of polish • Sponge • Nail tool • Gems • Nail glaze

THE COMPLETE LOOK

WHAT YOU'LL NEED

2 colors of polish • Nail tool • Mini pearls
• Gem • Nail glaze • Sponge

WINTER

THE COMPLETE LOOK

P. 17   P. 36

1 Paint on a clear base coat. Paint a blue stripe at the tip of your nail.

2 While the blue polish is still wet, blot it with the sponge to make a blue fade.

3 To paint the snowflake, start with three white stripes.

4 Add short white lines to make it look feathery.

5 Use glaze to attach pearls at the tips and a gem at the center of the snowflake.

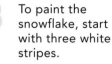

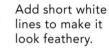

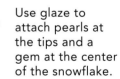

WHAT YOU'LL NEED

4 colors of polish • Nail tool • 2 gems
• Nail glaze • Triangle stud

OWL

1 Paint your nail a solid color.

2 Paint half of the nail a different color.

3 With the third color, paint a V shape at the base. Add small half-ovals on the sides for wings.

4 Use the dot tool to paint white circles for the eyes. Make small white dots on the chest.

5 Attach two gems with nail glaze to finish the eyes, and a triangle stud for a beak.

THE COMPLETE LOOK

P. 53

BUTTERFLY

WHAT YOU'LL NEED

2 colors of polish • Nail tool • Butterfly charms • Nail glaze

1

Paint your nail a solid color.

2

Add fluffy clouds with white polish.

3

Attach the butterfly charms with nail glaze.

THE COMPLETE LOOK

OCTOPUS

WHAT YOU'LL NEED

- 4 colors of polish
- Nail tool
- 2 black mini pearls
- White mini pearls
- Nail glaze

1 Paint your middle nail a solid color.

2 Draw a purple circle at the base of the nail.

3 Make the circle into a teardrop shape.

4 Using the tool, draw lines that come from the head.

5 Draw white circles for eyes and a black half-circle for the mouth. Add pink dots on the head.

6 Attach mini pearls with glaze to finish the eyes.

This design is meant to take up three nails on one hand. It's best to paint the octopus head on the middle fingernail.

THE COMPLETE LOOK

7

Paint your first and third fingernails a solid color.

8

Draw curvy lines and big swirls to make tentacles.

9

Attach mini pearls along the tentacles with nail glaze.

CREDITS

EDITORS: April Chorba and F. S. Kim

COVER DESIGNERS: April Chorba and Kristin Carder

INTERIOR DESIGNER: Rae Ann Spitzenberger

TECHNICAL ILLUSTRATORS: Monika Roe, April Chorba, and Owen Keating

PACKAGE DESIGNER: Owen Keating

PHOTOGRAPHER: Camille Tokerud

STYLIST: Wendy Oswald Kinney

BUYER: Vicky Eva

MANAGING EDITOR: Barrie Zipkin

CRAFTERS: Lesley Thelander and Adrianna Youngren

SPECIAL THANKS TO: Stacy Lellos, Netta Rabin, Hannah Rogge, and Stefan Haas-Heye

Get creative with more from KLUTZ

Looking for more goof-proof activities, sneak peeks, and giveaways? Find us online!

f Klutz Books   P Klutz Books   ▶ Klutz   🐦 @KlutzBooks   📷 @KlutzBooks

Klutz.com • thefolks@klutz.com • 1-800-737-4123